BROOKLYN NETS

ALL-TIME GREATS

BY TED COLEMAN

Book design by Jake Slavik
Cover design by Jake Slavik

Photographs ©: Brandon Dill/AP Images, cover (top), 1 (top); Mark Duncan/AP Images, cover (bottom), 1 (bottom); John Lent/AP Images, 4; Harry Harris/AP Images, 7; Paul Benoit/AP Images, 9; Ron Frehm/AP Images, 10; Alan Greth/AP Images, 13; Cliff Welch/Icon Sportswire, 15; Pablo Martine Monsivaisz/AP Images, 16; Lynne Sladky/AP Images, 19; Noah K. Murray/AP Images, 21

Press Box Books, an imprint of Press Room Editions.

ISBN
978-1-63494-600-1 (library bound)
978-1-63494-618-6 (paperback)
978-1-63494-636-0 (epub)
978-1-63494-652-0 (hosted ebook)

Library of Congress Control Number: 2022913239

Distributed by North Star Editions, Inc.
2297 Waters Drive
Mendota Heights, MN 55120
www.northstareditions.com

Printed in the United States of America
Mankato, MN
012023

ABOUT THE AUTHOR

Ted Coleman is a freelance sportswriter and children's book author who lives in Louisville, Kentucky, with his trusty Affenpinscher, Chloe.

TABLE OF CONTENTS

BARRY
24
Nets
24

CHAPTER 1

THE ABA YEARS

The Brooklyn Nets began life in 1967 as the New Jersey Americans. Point guard **Bill Melchionni** arrived two years later. By then, the team had moved to Long Island, New York, and was called the Nets. Melchionni ran the offense for the first playoff appearance in team history in the 1969–70 season.

The early Nets played in the American Basketball Association (ABA). By 1972, they had made their first ABA Finals. **Rick Barry** led the way. The smooth-shooting forward averaged more than 31 points per game in 1971–72.

STAT SPOTLIGHT

POINTS PER GAME

NETS TEAM RECORD

Rick Barry: 31.5 (1971–72)

And he rarely left the court. He played an average of 45 minutes per game.

Center **Billy Paultz** was a rebounding machine under the hoop. He also could be counted on to score. He retired as the team's leader in rebounds.

The ABA was an exciting league. It was known for high-flying dunk artists. No one dunked quite like **Julius Erving**. "Dr. J" changed the game of basketball. His amazing skills in the air dazzled fans. Erving spent only 1973–76 with the Nets. But he was ABA Most Valuable Player (MVP) in all three seasons.

In two of those three years, the Nets won the ABA championship. But Dr. J didn't do it alone. Paultz was there for one title. Melchionni was still there for both. Point guard **Brian Taylor** ran the offense for both championship teams.

He added great defense too. No ABA player had more steals in 1974–75.

Fellow guard "Super" **John Williamson** also helped the Nets to both titles. He later became the team's top scorer after Erving left.

The Nets joined the NBA in 1976–77. They moved to New Jersey a year later. Forward **Bernard King** was the team's first NBA Draft pick. He put up big scoring numbers for the Nets. But the Nets struggled in their new league.

COACH LOUGHERY

Kevin Loughery and Julius Erving both came to the Nets in 1973. Erving brought the talent on the court. Head coach Loughery made sure to use Erving as much as possible on offense. Loughery's aggressive style was the perfect fit for Erving's skills. Loughery was known for his intensity on the bench. He coached and won more games than any coach in Nets history.

NETS
22
RWE
KING
22

WILLIAMS
52
NETS
52

CHAPTER 2

ACROSS THE RIVER

The Nets used their top draft pick in 1981 on forward **Buck Williams**. Williams was Rookie of the Year that season. In his first six seasons, Williams missed just a single game. In fact, he played more games than any Net ever. He was also a strong shooter and played tough defense.

The 1981–82 season marked the first of five Nets playoff appearances in a row. Guard **Otis Birdsong** helped share the scoring load with Williams. That duo helped the Nets improve by

STAT SPOTLIGHT

CAREER GAMES

NETS TEAM RECORD

Buck Williams: 635

20 wins from 1980–81 to 1981–82. Injuries were the only thing that limited Birdsong's game.

In the middle of those Nets teams was center **Mike Gminski**. Gminski hauled down plenty of rebounds. And a lot of them came on the offensive end.

The Nets made a run of playoff appearances in the early 1990s. **Chris Morris** led the way. The forward was a steady Nets player for seven seasons. He averaged double figures in scoring each year.

The Nets selected forward **Derrick Coleman** with the first overall draft pick in

NETS
44
NETS
NETS
3
COLEMAN
44

1990. He was Rookie of the Year that season and never looked back. Coleman regularly averaged more than 20 points per game. He often chipped in more than 10 rebounds as well.

Guard **Drazen Petrovic** lit up scoreboards from the time he arrived in 1991. He was one of the best three-point shooters in team history. But Petrovic's promising career was cut short. He died in a car crash in 1993.

Kenny Anderson was a native of New York. He quickly found a home in New Jersey. The Nets

"CHOCOLATE THUNDER"

Center Darryl Dawkins played for the Nets for four full seasons. He stood nearly 7' tall and weighed 250 pounds. But Dawkins had no trouble getting up in the air. Dawkins had a lot of power. Sometimes his dunks could shatter the glass on the backboard. The league soon had to find new rims and glass that didn't break so easily.

made him their starting point guard in 1992–93. Anderson became a skilled playmaker and made an All-Star Game. But the Nets were still looking for a championship team.

SPALDING
NEW JERSEY
24
NETS
JEFFERSON
24

CHAPTER 3
BROOKLYN BOUND

The Nets began to build a strong team in the late 1990s. **Keith Van Horn** was a big reason why. The forward made the All-Rookie Team in 1998. By the 2000s, he was a key player on both ends of the floor.

Richard Jefferson did a bit of everything for the 2000s Nets. The forward could score, rebound, and pass. Jefferson formed a great duo with point guard **Jason Kidd**.

Kidd and Jefferson both came to the Nets in 2001. Kidd was already a star NBA point guard.

He led the league in assists twice with the Nets. Kidd propelled the Nets to their first NBA Finals in 2002. They went again in 2003.

In 2004, the Nets added one of the most exciting players in NBA history. **Vince Carter** was known for scoring and big dunks. Carter brought his "Vinsanity" style of play to New Jersey. He recorded some of the best scoring seasons in Nets history.

Despite the talent, the Nets couldn't win a title. Most of the core players were gone by the time the Nets drafted center **Brook Lopez** in 2008. Lopez went on to score more points than any other Nets player.

STAT SPOTLIGHT

CAREER POINTS

NETS TEAM RECORD

Brook Lopez: 10,444

Point guard **Deron Williams** ran the Nets offense in the early 2010s. He was the team's top playmaker when it moved to Brooklyn in 2012–13.

By 2019, **Kyrie Irving** was manning the point in Brooklyn. Like Kidd and Williams, Irving was already a star before joining the Nets. He soon became an All-Star in Brooklyn as well.

Irving teamed with **Kevin Durant** to create one of the league's star duos. The lanky forward was a former MVP and one of the best scorers in league history. He and Irving had the Nets in the playoffs each year. But they were still looking for that first NBA title.

SUPERSTAR OWNER

One of the Nets' owners might have been more famous than the players. Rapper Jay-Z bought a share of the Nets in 2004. He was a big reason why the team moved to Brooklyn, his hometown. He also helped design the team's new uniforms and logos. The rapper sold his shares in the Nets in 2013.

Webull
NETS
7
DURANT
7

TIMELINE

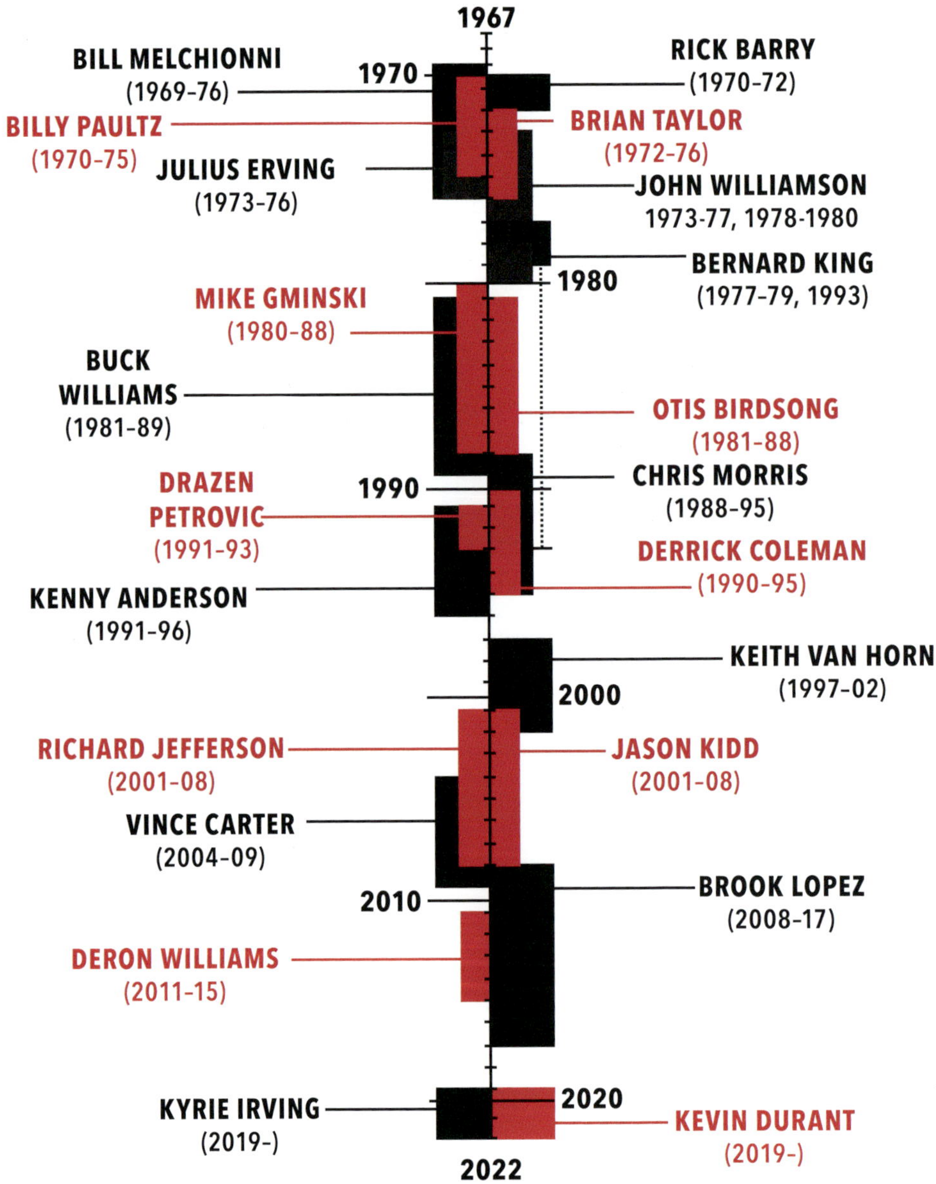
1967
BILL MELCHIONNI
(1969-76)
1970
RICK BARRY
(1970-72)
BILLY PAULTZ
(1970-75)
BRIAN TAYLOR
(1972-76)
JULIUS ERVING
(1973-76)
JOHN WILLIAMSON
1973-77, 1978-1980
BERNARD KING
(1977-79, 1993)
1980
MIKE GMINSKI
(1980-88)
BUCK
WILLIAMS
(1981-89)
OTIS BIRDSONG
(1981-88)
CHRIS MORRIS
(1988-95)
1990
DRAZEN
PETROVIC
(1991-93)
DERRICK COLEMAN
(1990-95)
KENNY ANDERSON
(1991-96)
KEITH VAN HORN
(1997-02)
2000
RICHARD JEFFERSON
(2001-08)
JASON KIDD
(2001-08)
VINCE CARTER
(2004-09)
BROOK LOPEZ
(2008-17)
2010
DERON WILLIAMS
(2011-15)
2020
KYRIE IRVING
(2019-)
KEVIN DURANT
(2019-)
2022

TEAM FACTS

BROOKLYN NETS

Formerly: New Jersey Americans (1967–68); New York Nets (1968–69 to 1976 77); New Jersey Nets (1977–78 to 2011–12)

First season: 1967–68

NBA championships: 0*

Key coaches:

Kevin Loughery (1973–74 to 1980)
297–318, 21–13 playoffs

Byron Scott (2000–01 to 2003–04)
149–139, 25–15 playoffs

MORE INFORMATION

To learn more about the Brooklyn Nets, go to **pressboxbooks.com/AllAccess**.

These links are routinely monitored and updated to provide the most current information available.

**Through 2021–22 season*

GLOSSARY

dazzled
Amazed others with an impressive skill.

draft
A system that allows teams to acquire new players coming into a league.

intensity
Showing extreme earnestness or seriousness.

playmaker
A player capable of setting up plays for others to score.

playoff
A set of games to decide a league's champion.

rookie
A first-year player.

INDEX